T0150169

Critical Acclaim for *Bootleg Sake*

"*I read it once… twice, every unexpected turn bringing joy. Bootleg Sake is the testament of a sophisticated sensualist with a firm, yet delicate touch. Erotic, bold, something new.*"
—Brandon Pitts, author of *Tender in the Age of Fury*

"Decadent, wry, and ripe with forbidden delight, *Bootleg Sake* is a fine brew for poetry lovers and pleasure seekers alike."
—Willow Loveday Little, author of *Xenia*

"*Exhibiting a puzzling knowledge of history and literary craftsmanship beyond what his years should permit. & Steeped. Exquisitely.in our troubled present time. With a face glancing toward humankind's Uncertain future. Devon Gallant's Bootleg Sake is a book for everyone! It's got something for us all.indeed. The floating world of Japan. BDSM. Hellenistic Splendor. Tender eroticism. Venetian & Roman fantasies and trysts. Deadheads. The darkness of Havana. Pearls of wisdom, and wistful remembrances… & More! This stunning. Full length book of poetry is something you are going to want, not only read, but revisit over, and over, again. & keep close at hand on your journey through this life.like a trusted. Amorous. sagacious …companion.*"
—Stedmond Pardy, author of *The Pleasure of this Planet Aren't Enough*

Critical Acclaim for *S(tars)* & *M(agnets)*

*"A paradoxical combination of simplicity and extravagance."*
———Allan Briesmaster, author of *The Long Bond:
Selected and New Poems*

*"These are the kinds of poems I see scholars at university take
time to study. I am stunned by what I am seeing."*
—Rudyard Fearon, author of *Free Soil*

*"s(tars) and m(agnets) a mirakul uv a book th narrator sails
flies thru galax eez in a bed uv stars brings his love cum thru fire
2 th prson celebrating n spreding within th birth uv unicorns each
lettr each beet each blessing is a book uv love uv daring 2 b now
writtn on an olympia typwritr th tactilitee uv each star each
moovment mesur brings a nu book uv joy 2 our opning hearts
devon gallant has dun sumthing reelee awesum n reelee
sewrapturous stedee xplorativ n radiant all within th wheel uv
time iuv usd selektid phrases from devon gallants writing 2
illustrate th wundrs n powrs uv th word magik heer"*
—bill bissett, author of *peter among th towring
boxes / text bites*

# Bootleg Sake

Library and Archives Canada Cataloguing in Publication

Title: Bootleg sake / Devon Gallant.

Names: Gallant, Devon, author.

Description: Poems.

Identifiers: Canadiana (print) 2022017301X | Canadiana (ebook) 20220174431 | ISBN 9781771616447 (softcover) | ISBN 9781771616454 (PDF) | ISBN 9781771616461 (EPUB) | ISBN 9781771616478 (Kindle)

Classification: LCC PS8613.A459365 B66 2022
DDC C811/.6—dc23

Published by Mosaic Press, Oakville, Ontario, Canada, 2022

MOSAIC PRESS, Publishers

www.Mosaic-Press.com

Printed and bound in Canada.

Cover Design by Bianca Cuffaro and Devon Gallant

Interior Page Design by Devon Gallant

MOSAIC PRESS
1252 Speers Road, Units 1 & 2, Oakville, Ontario, L6L 5N9
(905) 825-2130 • info@mosaic-press.com • www.mosaic-press.com

# Bootleg Sake

# Devon Gallant

For Bianca

Also by Devon Gallant

S(tars) & M(agnets) | 2015

His Inner Season | 2012

the flower dress and other lines | 2009

The Day After | 2006

*"I am the director of love and freedom."*
—Takashi Miike

*"I have a one-track mind.*
*That's all I'm interested in, is love."*
—John Cassavetes

# TABLE OF CONTENTS

# I

# II

*"The tale of how the first truly SM oriented magazines began publishing in Japan can be somewhat garbled depending on who's telling the story but the outlines are fairly consistent. After the war there appeared a number of what we in the West would call 'pulp magazines' catering to various interests. These were wryly called 'kasutori' ('bootleg sake' or 'low grade liquor' because of the cheap paper on which they were printed and because of their often vaguely salacious and erotic content."*
   —*from* The Beauty of Kinbaku

*"Don't believe anyone's BS 100%, not even your own. And by BS, I mean Belief System."*
   —Robert Anton Wilson

**I**

# YOUNG PINES

Let us embrace the beauty of this moment.

It is autumn
and the chrysanthemum reaches out,
yearning for embrace.

It is spring
and the cherry blossom poises its lips,
like a lover waiting for their first, shy kiss.

It is summer
and lavender exalts in the field
with erotic ardor.

Whatever the season may be,
the flowers of love abound.

Incorrigibly,
we surrender:
        in the secluded corners of shady tea rooms,
        in isolated bath houses
        along the far edges of the city,
        down the disused, dusty corridors
        of some forgotten palace hall.

We are young pines at play—
young still—and we must savor the sanctity
of this moment:
        enveloped in a parade of silks,
        the books and games cast aside,
        the sake gone cold.

Nothing in life matters as much as this
and the warmth of us in wanton indulgence

on a lazy afternoon.

# A PICTURE OF SPRING

Venus and Mars lay shackled to the bed.
Caught, in their amorous love-play,
by that deformed, old cuckold, Vulcan.
Who had fastened invisible fetters
to each of the four corners
of their concupiscent haven.
(The old dungeon master!)

The gods all come to laugh:
"Naughty, naughty!" and
"Is that Mars I see retreating from the field of battle?"
and other such jests, all in good fun.
Jupiter with perhaps just a touch more than sympathy
in his watering eyes.

Vulcan is enraged, to be sure,
but is that all?
How long did he lurk there, in the shadows,
before the trap was sprung?
The shame and humiliation washing over him
as he gazed upon those two lovers—irreparably entwined—
immaculate in their reciprocal beauty.
Did some strange, unspeakable flame
arouse itself in that malformed god of fire?
Devouring their carnal fervor
like some perverted fantasy come alive.
The scenario pre-arranged all the while
by dedicated wife, voyeuristic husband.

Oh yes, tears shall pour tonight,
but from what fount shall they spring?

Reconciliation will come
and reparations be made—
Venus on her knees, repentant.

      "You've been a bad girl."
      "Yes, Master."

Both knowing the cycle will repeat itself,
ad infinitum.

I, for one, have no need of Vulcan iron
to make me a prisoner of your bed.
For you have been and always will be
my one true Goddess of Love.

Nevertheless, if, on those nights when I come,
spear in hand, looking to conquer,
you find yourself aflamed
by the thought of some jealous god in the shadows...
my dear, you are the sovereign of your own mind.

For, when we are bound in sinful abandon,
the fire of our love burns away all impurities,
a transmutation of the soul.

And whether through ordeal or delight,
we unite in the alchemy of our love.

# ARS MEMORIA

Come: enter the theatre of my mind.
Like Giulio Camillo, I invite you
to step away from the bustling Venetian waterways—
the charismatic, swarthy gondoliers;
the mask vendors, merchants, and friars;
rival factions of pundits and academics—
and transcend onto a higher plane of awareness.

You are not stranger nor spectator here.

I place you with me at the center of the stage
and together we stare out
at the wonders of the universe.

All art is, in some way, an art of memory.
An attempt to preserve, not just the experience,
but the complex essence of that experience.
Fact and fiction merged.

Before you know it, it's gone, lost forever.
We're shadows living in a shadow world.
Our memories the only elusive trace
that we ever lived, breathed, existed
in anything remotely resembling Now.

Memory is the pillar which holds aloft our reality.

Without memory we are blind, soul-blind,
in a merciless land of cliffs.

My poems are the imagines agentes
that lead us both
along an ever ascending trail

to cosmos of illumination and colossal expanse.

# WHEN YOU TOUCH YOURSELF

When you touch yourself, think only of me.
Let your fingers pressed
be my lips, licking hard
against your clit.

Let the sweat that collects
across your thighs and breasts
be the saliva from my searching tongue.

Pinch your nipples,
thinking only of my biting teeth.

For, in the desperate, eroticism of my solitude,
I think only of you—

your lips around my cock,
your breasts heaving across my chest,
your sticky wet cunt
trailing across my skin—

as I beat, angrily, for consolation.

Waiting for the return
of your arching back

and the impenetrable beauty
of your arcane eyes.

# THE RITE OF SUBMISSION

## I. THE ADORATION OF THE FLESH

Bashful and ardent, you tied a cord 'round my arm—
aquamarine, as the color of your dress—
called it a 'memento amore'
to ward against the Spirits of the Night.
Said, "Godspeed!" and that was that, I was off,
down an uncertain path towards perilous new tomorrows—
rocky and grey, summer gone—
with little more than steadfast resolve
and the faint promise of amorous concord—
diffused through the stratus of newly-wintered clouds—
to keep me safe and sane.

The memory of you transfixed in my mind:
the delicate robins of your hands,
the pressure of blood
beneath cinched cord,
the carols of sunlight in your hair,
the diamond sparkle of tears—
making your eyes seem even more magical,
even more devastating and undeniable.

The Quest. The Proof of Love.
What a child's games we played.
What an infantile charade of chivalry.

How could we have comprehended
the trials I would face?
The ordeals encountered?

How could we have anticipated
the terrible toll of this wayward wandering?
Or the reckless ruination of the rambling road
on a banished heart?

Lost. Astray.
A vagabond pledged to a sojourn known only to us two.
Compelled, forlornly, through the deepest recesses
of unconsummated desire.

Derelict. Abandoned.
Adrift on an odyssey given no finite bounds
besides the undisclosed weight of your heart—
placed, precariously, on a scale
between capricious affection and physical decay.

At crossroads unknown
and back alleys unseen,
I met evil.
Evil no language can account for.
Evil no earth can bear.

Poisoned, tricked, tortured, defiled;
I became a beggar, haggard and worn.

And yet, all the while, I thought of you.
You infused the landscape around me.
You emanated from the sparkle of stars, the rustle of leaves,
the glow of the fire.

I worshiped the faintest trace of you.

But, did you think of me?
Did you dream, daily, of my return?

For, one day, I will return.
Like the spring blossom, I will burgeon
from this ruined land of waste

renewed, reinvigorated, reborn.

## II. THE CEREMONY

But, of course, the nights grow long, don't they?
Winter arrives—uninvited guest— heaping whatever
portions you have left of...joy, exuberance, hope...
onto its greedy plate. The sun's passing glimpse
too polite to linger.

You strive to preserve the memory of it—
the heartfelt ardor of your promise—
but without even the furtive remembrance
of a stolen kiss to hold onto, it slips away.
Leaving only the vague ideal
of what was and one day might be.

It is a frail image to place within your Palace of Things,
and as the years unravel, it withers
like the nose on an old Roman bust.

An honorable maiden tries to resist,
but how many bouquets can be returned demurely?
How many elaborate banquets forgone
before the deep belly-ache sets in?
A hunger to be encompassed by not just one particular,
but any set of arms available.
How many days must pass in neglect
before, finally, you succumb to the Master's bedroom?

Beeswax illuminates ornate tapestries
of Pan, Hecate, and Aphrodite.
Lining the walls in their illicit narratives
through the candle-lit glow.

Plums stewed in rose-water
and pears poached in wine
lay in wait on a silver tray
beside chilled bottles of
Cypriot, Muscatel, and Grenache.

The silk scarf envelopes you in darkness.
The rough touch of damask grazing your flesh—
naked, except for the tightly drawn corset.
The rattle of dungeon things quivers in your ears.
The sharp sting of leather
as it kisses the tender mouth of back.

Although it startles you, you feel cherished.
Your body a sacred text, illuminated manuscript.
A book of hours where every inch is...
studied, relished, rarefied.
Becoming something new, unknown.
Yielding to new and forbidden desires
as you ascend, ever higher, into radical plateaus
of pleasure and pain.
Liberated through the oppression,
you submit, body and soul,
to this Emissary of Terrors.

And where is your knight errant now,
to save you from this dragon?
Off on some crusade you'll never reckon
or give credence to again.

Let courtly love suffice for the frigid and faint of heart,
this maiden has found a new doctrine to ascribe to.

"Let us drink," he says, pouring wine
        through parted lips.
"Let us play," he says, dripping wax
        onto quivering bosom.
"Let us walk out into the starlit fields of our dark desire,
        alive in the leaves and trees and grass.
        I, horned god. You, moon goddess.
Oceans of hands raining down in infinite devotion."

# RIGHT HAND TWILL

Tokubei wore his pair of Big John's wherever he went.
Claimed they were the first pair of KD-8s ever made.
     "Your jeans are filthy." Ohatsu said.
     "For the fade," was all he replied.
He had drifted into Osaka sometime in the early 70s,
lurking around the local pachinko parlors—
his dog-eared copy of Lone Wolf and Cub
hanging from the back pocket of his jeans.
Nobody knew much about him,
although there were rumours he had taken part
in the student protests of '68
and was expelled from university in Tokyo.

Ohatsu wasn't sure what she wanted from life.
She knew she didn't the want the life her mother had had.
She didn't want any part of the "Three Submissions,"
gentile tea ceremonies, or cleaning house.
She didn't want a normal life.
And something about Tokubei
promised her that much, at least.

It wasn't until the women's liberation march
down Dotonbori that he noticed her, glistening with sweat,
eyes gleaming, chanting: "Sei-no-kaiho! Sei-no-kaiho!"
He cruised up to her in his Yamaha XS1,
pulled out an old issue of Kitan Club:
     "Looking for liberation?" He asked.
They made love under the stars that night
amd every night after and she found the liberation
she was looking for, just not in the way she expected.

Tokubei taught her about a fourth submission,
a submission to desire:
"Everything has a spirit," he said.
"The stars, the grass, this rope, my jeans."
Wrapping her naked body in the long jute rope.

"These bodies are mortal, but our spirit lives on."
The weft of the transverse thread looping over the warp
of the longitudinal. Her body bound
in an interlacing web of weaves,
like the right hand twill of Tokubei's Big John's.
"Who are we? Why are we alive? What is our destiny?
Like my jeans, the character of our souls reveals itself
only through time and use. Like the cherry blossom,
our lives are fleeting, but given poignancy and power
through this...inevitable...defeat..."
Tokubei and Ohatsu shivering together in unified orgasm,
like reeds in the wind.

"Who wants to work the same job
the rest of their life anyway?
All this talk about harmony, but they don't get it.
There's no harmony in conformity.
It's only when things oppose each other—Yin and Yang.
Harmony is about Chaos, not Order."

Pretty soon, the other students began following Ohatsu
down the hall: "When are you two going to suicide!"
And then, during the festival of the Harvest Moon
a gang of boys cornered Tokubei by the arcades
and beat him to within an inch of his life.

"Let's get out of here, Ohatsu. There's a whole world
these people aren't ever going to understand.
I'm never going to let them hammer me down,
no matter how hard they try."

And so, not dead but still reborn,
Tokubei and Ohatsu left Osaka.
Blazing down the freeway,

screaming dissident fireworks towards a rarified jubilee.

# EROGURONANSENSU

What sleeping beauty
waits here, with razor-blade lips?
Where is the angel
I travelled so far to find?
Who has replaced her
with this spoilt, undead corpse?
When will my cherub
return, with her star-bright eyes,
to the meadow of our love?

How I remember
our nights tenderly embrace.
Your warm, dewey tongue
on the belly of my cock.
My hands sticky wet
with that sweet pollen of life.
The rosebud of ass,
our fingers intermingled,
blooming to all inquiry.

Yet, now I behold
this fearful facsimile
in whose raven black
hair is crawling with lice,
whose pearlescent pale skin
devastated with maggots
and I am gripped
with a revolting horror
as though covered in shit.

"Zebra dicks!" I cry.
Which, of course, awakens her;
letting out a howl
that arouses her hag mass.
Terrified, I run,
chased across an ashen land,
thinking only: "Please,
oh God, don't let me become a
sex slave to these hell hags."

# PANACEA

Although Mankind runs, ever fearful,
from that pale rider, Death—
scouring the globe for some hidden key
to save them from their reckoning—

I have no need for secret salvation.

From the dusky plains of the Sonoran desert
to the verdant hills along the river Yangtze:
there is no elixir of life—no poultice or potion—
that can compare to the rejuvenation of your love.

I spent years lost in a mad quest—
searching for the Fountain of Youth,
the Philosopher's Stone;
drinking gold and eating jade;
trawling the ocean floor for Amrita
and the lost city of Atlantis—

I raced through the night,
chasing the white rabbit
for the secrets of the moon;
exchanged tales of adventure and woe
in the back of too many pubs to count—
bleary-eyed and mouth-sour
from whiskey and heart-ache.

I joined the ranks of life extensionists,
immortalists,
longevists,
cyborgs,
all desperate for some agerasia,
some negligible senescence,
to fill the void of their broken souls.

I dreamed of an oncoming singularity—
a digital ascension—
to lose myself in techno-submission;
uploading my brain into a cloud-based Nirvana.

All the while, never realizing:
there was no Holy Grail
that did not lie between your thighs:

"Whoever drinks the water I give him will never thirst."

Let the world go on in its futile hunt for immortality,
neither Soma nor Somatropin can compare
to the dancing waters of your eyes,
the curative cleanse of your kiss,

a kiss
which tastes
like a peach,

       soft and sweet,

in the morning rain.

# TIDE JEWELS

But, of course, the pearls were always just a pretext;
a veiled rationale to enter the Forbidden Kingdom.

Moonlight sparkling beneath cascading waves—
the refracted light slowly filtered of its warmer tones.
Drawn towards the faint serenade of...
flute, oboe, campanello...the melodious choir of
undulating sevenths, diminished and minor.
The tuxedo-clad glamour of orchestra and conductor
encased in crystal; the concert hall: coral red and white—
because, after all, it is always a Grand Affair
in the palace of the Dragon King.

As a child, they used to frighten her
with tales of crooked things in the dark—
the bleeding breast of Tamatori.

> (If Man could not soar to the Sun,
> then Woman could not plunge to the depths.)

But, in her heart, always she knew:
she was a Woman of the Sea.

There was the promise of the twin jewels—ebb and flow—
that had toppled nations, granted wishes...
bequeathed immortality.

Their fear saw it as a trespass.
Thus, the hyperbole: shokushu goukan.

But, in truth, it was an invitation,
an escape.

A reprieve from the codified oppression
that awaited...
                    above the water.

A release, a return
to something deeper even
than her animistic self.
Something even more ancient and enigmatic.

Of course, it was taboo. That was the thrill.

       (Isn't it always?)

Her own private Xanadu
where untold pleasures awaited.
Her mind and body torn between sex and survival,
while eight (sixteen if you're lucky) industrious
tentacles attended her every whim.
Catapulting her to a level of erotic transcendence
that verged upon ego death, a dissolution of the self,
a glimpse into the Pure Land...Nirvana.

But, let's not forget about Mr. Octopus!
For he, also, has his own drama to contend with:
the classic male dilemma of premature ejaculation.

Lost in the pleasure of his work,
he must never forget to hold back the hectocotylus
or he will die.

And although he is greatly enamored
with this foreign beauty
who has deigned to grace his seabed,
he recognizes, as well, that she is not exaclty
a girl-to-bring-home-to-mother.

No, they must be transparent about their little tryst.
Each knowing it is one of those fleeting moments
made all the more bittersweet
by the macabre ballet they pirouette between life and death.

A Romeo and Juliet, if you will.

(And why not?)

Two star-struck lovers from polar cosms—
each inexplicably drawn to each—
locked in a quasi-shinju impulse.
Pushing the boundaries just a little further each time.

In the pious dawn, she will resurface,
clutching her handful of pearls.
Slipping her cold, wet body beside her fisherman husband.
Bequeath brackish kisses on his dormant lips.
Her tongue, itself like a tentacle,
probing the moist, warm cavern of his mouth
until, aroused from his slumber,
he gazes up upon his Empress-Queen
sparkling in the last glimmers of starlight.

> Kings and queens adorn themselves in pearls—
> a kaleidoscopic raiment of hues, from black to white—
> yet, they remain ever ignorant
> of the true treasure they hold:
> not of baubles, but of souls
> who found for themselves, however briefly,
> an oasis of comfort
>
> in the vast desert of isolated acquiescence.

# BROACHING THE SUBJECT

I would reveal to you my thesis,
but what's the fun in that?

Let's tease meaning;
                  dual bound
                  to the forward play
                  of these cunning linguistic gropes.

I fear you live by an ideology
and it has made you cold and callous.
While I, live by my senses.
Following the world
like a dog at play—
                  your best friend
                  and obedient servant.

Place a collar around me,
if you will.
            I will submit.
And yet, something in me remains
of the stars and grass,
and the bristle of the midnight wind.

I would share this with you, if you let me.

We might learn from each other.
I, eating from your hand, teacher's pet.
Looking up with adoring eyes to your stern discipline.
You, re-living your youth,
wondering where it all went wrong.

Both knowing
that the student invariably becomes
the Master.

# FESTIVAL OF STARS

"...but I digress. The point is, I, for one, have never been
so offended by some so-called 'patch of purple.'
Without wishing to affront the authoritas of Horace—
what is poetry if not one gigantic patch of purple
in the ever evolving tableau of human history?
It's almost as foolish as Emerson's diatribe
against 'French coffee.' The real question is: what is a poet?
For centuries, great minds have championed poets
as semi-divine oracles—Bocaccio claiming poetry proceeded
from the 'bosom of God,' Ronsard avowing that Muses reside
solely in a soul that is 'saintly' and 'virtuous.'
For myself, I cannot look upon any poet, living or dead,
as anything more or less than human: flawed to a greater
or less degree, talented to a greater or less degree.
If, I myself, have donned the role of shaman at times,
I must adhere to that indefatigable truth: that
roles and souls are different realms of the same individual.
I would not ask a reader to deify me, for I am no saint.
And nor do I believe any artist is.
Art may very well be the road to self-discovery,
but roads have a length and a destination.
Simply being on them does not mean you have arrived.

So, what is poetry? An elusive question at any time,
but in our age, even more so. The answers passed down to us
fall flat in our modern era. Sidney's oft-quoted paean:
'to teach and delight,' feels ridiculous
when applied to poetry—to Art as a whole maybe, but
the truth is, no one reads poetry anymore. For either
teaching or delighting. No, as Peacock predicted, we have
become irrelevant—and not because of the abundance
of poetry already written. For, as Emerson writes:
'each new age requires a new confession,'
and I have always believed that the best art created
from any art form must necessarily be
its present day manifestation.

Eliot was quite right when he said the 'existing order'
re-adjusts to make room for the new.
Vico, Peacock, Bloom...I cannot understand
these arrogant men who see the evolution of poetry
as a spiral of descent, a trajectory of decay,
with ever diminishing returns.
They value the works of Homer and Virgil too greatly
and lack imagination for the possibilities of the future.

So, what is a poem? To me, it is simply a genre.
One that has fallen out of favour with the majority of people
living today; written by and for a small minority.
I am trepidatious to bequeath it any more power than that.
Perhaps, it is true, I have tried, as Mazzoni, to reach
beyond the appearance of reality. To grasp at the 'impossible
things' beyond it. Or, like Vico, to retain my childish wonder;
transcribe it with a 'robust sense and vigourous imagination.'
To 'lift the veil from the hidden beauty of the world,'
as Shelley writes, and pour out with Wordsworth's
'spontaneaous overflow of powerful feelings.' Regardless,
I refuse to impose my own bias on another. At one time,
I believed, as Horace, that poetry should be
'simple and unified,' but this brought me no success in life.
Times and tastes change and whether or not poetry
'must be difficult,' poets must certainly be versatile.
What is poetry? Only the future can answer that.

I still remember the day when my mentor told me
that I would surpass her one day. She said this was a good
and natural thing. Mind you, this was not something
that I consciously desired. I had always imagined us
kindred souls who would grow old and support each other
over time. Unlike what Bloom may believe, I have never
suffered from any great 'anxiety of influence.' Perhaps,
it is my femininity which sets me apart from this world of
male aggression. Certainly, I searched for the deeper music
of poetry. Could we call this Kristeva's genotext?

Was I attempting to return to some pre-Oedipal
state of mind? Groping my way back to a pre-linguistic
sense of womb safety? I cannot say. What I can say,
is that when I did finally surpass her, I realized the loneliness
of that victory. Most writers desire to be innovators, but
very few realize what a terrifying prospect that can be:
to be adrift, without a guiding light, yet knowing there is still
so far to go. Now that I am old, I pray for somebody to come
and show me the way, so that I won't be so alone, anymore.
So that I'll be able to see the way again. Once more amazed,
once more astonished..."
                                        As Komachi trails off, she watches
the young girl dance by the fire. Becoming transfixed
by the gyrating limbs in the flames.
She rises and joins her; dancing to the music
of the festival with her eyes closed.
Succumbing to the music.

When she finally opens her eyes again, the girl is gone.
She walks out of the tent and sees young lovers
carousing in the dawn light of the meadow,
and is suddenly filled with shame and heartache.

She was beautiful once, but she wielded that beauty
like a katana
                and now she is alone.

The sun is rising and the festival decorations
swim in the wind. A dazzling array
of seeds bound for what soil?
She approaches a tree adorned in hopes and dreams.
Finds a scrap of paper, writes a poem, and
ties it to the tree.
She closes her eyes and listens to the morning birds,
heralding a new dawn.

Awakened, once more, from the dark domain.

# MY UNICORN WILL MAKE ALIVE EVERY NEED

though mysterious
I catch a delicate wonder
which would never
pursue her fabulous chaste garden

legend has it there rides a unicorn,
prancing, wandering, strong

playful mount
ferocious rainbow
lie but through primeval play
this maiden kingdom
is out to tame
while we alone sparkle free

quest, myth
this is about escape
run noble beast if you must
our each solitary strength
deep aphrodisiac

you, selfless woman
I, honest man
forever wild
always gold

she caught full of all that was
turned off virtue or fear
lay by moon creatures
as was her wont
leapt some then captured, whitely

his true star wish

# MERCY

And as bees ingest nectar and cows secrete milk,
so too, do I wish to produce in your service.
Yet, how may I transform myself into such ilk
when flooding through these veins runs a hot-blooded vice?

Yes, I am the white bull of desire and lust pours
through me. But hailing from where? Heaven or Hell?
For, though I am determined to be only yours,
my devotion falters as though under a spell.

Each night, I dream of a bejeweled succubus,
deft in the supple arts of feline seduction.
Fulfilling all wishes, a naked enchantress
who lifts me away, relieving all affliction.

Is it wrong to succumb to fervid fantasy?
Frolicking in the garden of its strange delight?
Then, why this urge, placed so deep inside of me?
Though I claw it out with smutted hands, black as night.

Oh Goddess, with your penetrant eyes ablaze,
I would gladly grant you a barrel of my blood
if only you would transfigure that dreadful gaze
and, with kinder eyes, let your benevolence flood.

Guide me, like the river that runs to the ocean.
Teach me the magic of your luminescent moon.
Reveal the secret of your bhaktic devotion
to one who searches for spiritual commune.

Goddess of love, abduct me to your strange new shores.
Show me a way to harness this awesome power.
Never placing between us what nature abhors.
Our union blooming, our love a cosmic flower.

Reach out and hold me with your wealth of hands, Lakshmi,
for I am mired deep in the swamp of my sin.
And though I wish to be a poem of mercy
where should I start, if not this poor alexandrine?

# FLOATING WORLD

## I.

Day upon sorrowful day:
penniless, in rags, ravenous,
nothing to eat
but one rice ball after another,
bland, choked down with tears,
aching feet, tired, broken back,
showing more years than the passage of time can account for,
years accrued in suffering and loss, tallied by...
lack, need, want...the paddy fields, relentless,
taking every hour of the waking day, no end in sight,
aging parents, breaking down, dependent,
the sake-filled nights of drunken refuge
few and far between,
the cherry blossoms distant, the swans flown,
your heart, isolated and cold as Mount Fuji.
Suffocated with the irrepressible sense
that you are little more than a puppet on a string,
the book held aloft, the tragedy faithfully rendered,
no deviations allowed from the script.

Is it any wonder you dreamed of entering the floating world?

Where play replaced production,
and parade replaced pain.

The streets an opulent canvas of perfume, kimonos,
and white-moon faces.

Then, there was her.

You were broken and remade the moment you saw her.

Azuma.

## II.

But, of course, your feelings
were only part of the equation, weren't they?

What about her?
Her love? Her desire?

The tortuous years of training,
navigating the dark alleys of the yukaku,
averting the grasping hands of untold perverts,
scared, away from home, unloved, uncherished,
holding the tobacco box in the corner
as she watches her future play out in front of her:
drooling, callous men hedging in on the 'wily' courtesan.
Then the years of powerlessness that followed,
when she couldn't say no, to anyone, forced
to share her bed with any grease-filled palm with gold,
the right to choose, a hard fought victory,
paid for in degradation and shame,

and although the cowardice
of the one she has chosen
has kept her in bondage,
you make a promise to yourself,

a vow to her and her moonbright-face.

Leaving the rice fields of Osaka
for the oil fields of Edo
in an odd-even gamble of life and love,

to free your darling Azuma.

## III.

In the end,
all it cost was 300 gold coins
and a broken heart

and she is free
to seek out her joy
and sadness
in whatever far-flung field of her own choosing.

Yet, although her strings are cut,
you wallow, still,
against the fabricated backdrop.

Dissonant, guttural singing intertwined
with plucked shamisen,
as unseen hands
direct your every sorrow.

Igniting the audience in torrential applause.

# AMATERASU

All the beasts of the forest cry for her
yet, to their pleading, she will demur.
For, as with any heart betrayed, this lioness
must elude into the wilderness.
Nothing being ever so fragilely adorned
as the tears of a lover scorned.

We took for surety her proudful splendor—
frolicking, gayly, beneath her centre.
Never a care to what storm might approach;
trusting a brother to heed his sister's reproach.
But now, the skies gone black, we must
fumble blindly into this world we're thrust.
Carrying on, stoic and brave,
as she recedes into her heavenly cave.

Tell me, what bard might with song enchant
or king with riches grant
a relief for our grieving goddess?
Men haunt these woods, a rag tag chorus,
yet, one by one, they depart unrequited
and all despair the world blighted.
Until, Lady Dawn arrives, irreverent and crude,
gyrating in a sapphic bounty none find rude.

# STILETTO S.

For now, the world outside is a mystery left unresolved.
These could be the last minutes till midnight,
our magic is stronger than the cuckoo's cry.
Gilded carriage? Pumpkin?
It hardly matters what awaits you
on that long, dark voyage home,
I have found you, you are mine.

When I was king of both sand and sun
an eagle dropped a slipper onto my lap.
Was this the beginning, my rosy-cheeks?
I feel as though I have found and lost and found you
over and over, time and again.
Prince. King.
Full of riches but poor in love,
clutching that single piece of the puzzle,
just trying to make it fit.

But if I suffered from a surfeit of riches, you labored
under the burden of a boundless affection.
An unfathomable weight which dragged you
into the foul crevices of life's tragic menagerie.
Ashen were the roads that led you to me,
but in your heart, always, you remained spotless.
Oh courtesan, with flowers in your hair,
reclined on velvet divan,
although this world has persecuted your beauty,
you are pure equine aristocracy, bourgeois extravagance,
the embodiment of all the frivolity
this world has lost, yet so desperately needs.

I dreamed of you then, those long nights from home.
Back when the world fell apart
and we were just trying to put it all together again.
'Glory seekers' they called us, 'princes of the sky,'
but inside we were just boys—scared, nerves shot—
taking it day by day, knowing it could end at any moment.

After Schweinfurt, knowing it all too well.
The Luftwaffe, a force to be reckoned with.
Their single pusher, caliber 40 chronographs
giving them an edge,
German engineering at its finest.

But amidst the bombs and bullets and screaming metal,
you were there—
                        pinned up in kodachrome perfection,
                        Betty Grable style,
                        contrapposto,
                        a coy smile over your shoulder,
                        buttocks poised,

with nothing on but a swimsuit and heels.

I'll always remember that night in California,
drunk on cocktails we'd never heard of before.
How I told you it was all going to be okay
and you kissed me, tasting of rum, limes and sugar.
The Pacific never looked better
than that night at the back of Donn's.

When I landed on the shores of Salerno,
I made a promise to bring you there one day.
Get drunk on Campari, and sail to Capri,
just like in the song.
You were what kept me alive, what I fought for.
Both as an ideal and as a tangible reward.
A well-earned prize for a hard-fought victory.

But if the world seemed to me a nightmare,
it was no darker than the dance you danced,
night after night. Thrust into the limelight...6, 7, 8
inches above the ground. Adorned in crystal clear heels,
but still waiting for Prince Charming to arrive.

Those days are behind us now, but we find ourselves
still caught in the narrative:
> Persecuted heroine.
> Rescuing prince.
>
> Degradation and salvation.
> (With me, pulling double duty!)

It is a private game we play
for our own amusement.

You no longer a Cinderella, but a Sinderella.
Donning your Christian Dior's like twin talismans,
digging them into my chest
with the precision of a Venetian assassin.

Don't ask me whether it glorifies or demeans,
whether I am placing you on a pedestal
or tearing you down from one.

All I know,
is that when you come to me
adorned in heels,

you are a lioness

tame, untameable

wild, transcendent, sublime.

My sweet, sweet Stiletto S.

# OUROBOROS

King Tut is born again: Osiris volleying back to Amun-Ra.
(What else is there to do with all that sand?)
Never again to be Sun God or saint,
never again to build castles in the sand,
but alive, nevertheless, in the here and present Now.

We are kings and queens all, are we not?
The blank canvas of our past lives an open invitation
for poetic license. Our collective amnesia
a convenient excuse to disregard the mundane existences:
the baby-makers, soil tillers, salt-of-the-earth alcoholics...
bankers...cashiers...

But in the end, it all comes back to kink.
The collar, the shackles, the coiled whip:
all emblems for the snake eating its own tail. Ourobos.
The sinuous tension of Life and Death,
Creation and Destruction, Yin and Yang,
all tied-up into one alluring package.
It is more than just procreation.
No amount of burning books could quell it.
No amount of dogma could silence it.
We are the chaos that breaks the order we create. Ouroboros.
The snake eating its own tail.

Maybe this all sounds like I ascribe to some type of
antiquated ideal: supplicant woman, dominant man—
Beauty and the Beast—but that's not it at all.
I simply believe: that whenever two souls join together,
whoever they are, that above the hot, sweaty, musk
of sex and licentiousness, they are able to unpack
some of that weird, terrible, mixed-up baggage,
lay it out, look at it,
then fold it back just a little neater till next time.
Till the cycle repeats. Ouroboros.

Till King Tut is born again.

# CALLE DEI FABBRI

Thrust into the chaogical splendor of the Piazza San Marco;
mesmerwelmed by the ornate Byzantine basilica—
as dizzying to the eye as the flooding rush of bodies,
storming in constant frenetergy. Searching
for a street so near and yet, somehow, so far.

Somewhere, Calle dei Fabbri awaits
    around the corner you didn't take,
    across the bridge you just missed, gondolost
    in the meantricate web that is Venice.

A city no map can trace.
Winding and wonderphorical,
twisting and turning ever onwards
to new passages of touristic delight. Roads,
both inward and outward,
of self-discovery and soul-surrender.

Stumbling though the idyllic, jagged alleys of Dorsoduro,
you gaze into the quaint boutiques selling Venetian masks.
Fantasize about secret, bourgeois, European orgies,
you'll never attend, or even be invited to.

(Full moon at the height of Carnival: the full, voluptuous
breasts and long, high-heeled legs of Esmeralda as she
leads you down the palace corridor
of some lesser Italian prince, naked,
except for the black velvet cape and gold eagle-headed mask.
Orgasming almost instantly and then surrendering
to the ravenous wave of flesh, undulating
like one more piece of flotsam in the tepid sea of sex.
Lubricated by semen, sweat, saliva; between your teeth,
coating your tongue, tucked in the corners of your eyes,
armpits, toes...awaking the next morning, searching
for her amongst the fishmongers and hurried eyes
of travelers, hoping for some sixth sense to blossom within,
imploring into each pair of lost eyes you meet.)

Next, you arrive at the Campo Santa Margherita,
steal yourself a piece of heaven on an open terrazzo.
Pound back one Aperol Spritz, and another,
and watch the sun go down,
bathing the cobblestone square
in a profusion of rose, peach, and violet.
Listen to the children play and dogs bark
as you breathe in the unspeakable beauty around you.

It's a long way to travel for a wine cocktail.

Venice, a utopia in the truest sense
for it truly is no place at all, a Disneyland for the soul,
where you lose yourself searching
for that 'authentic Italian experience.'
You leave feeling both have evaded you,
yet still being richer for the experience.

I came to Venice searching for a time machine.
Attempting to find something that was long gone.
I came looking for you, Vincent Price,
your sense of joy and wonder, your love of humanity.
And I found it. Not at the Royal Danieli, or the Cafe Florian,
or Harry's Bar. Not by following your footsteps,
but by following your heart.

I came with pennies to the land of gold,
but couldn't bring myself to hate the opulence.
For, isn't it what we all strive to achieve? A life well lived?
And who is it, I spy, in the lobbies of those five star hotels,
dining on truffles and caviar
from their panoramic rooftop gardens?
Aren't they just another traveler
trapped in this sandbox of life?

Each carrying a portmanteau, neatly packed
with their own allotted share of joy and misery,
awaiting the next destination.
                         —Venezia 2017

# DAVID

Arriving at the Santa Maria Novela in Florence,
all those old anxieties from Havana come
bubbling back to the surface.

Florence exudes the same sense of melancholy as that city.
It shimmers with the same haunted memory
of a city that was once brilliant.

Approaching the Duomo,
it's easy to understand how Gothic horror
was born from these imposing structures.
(A city caught in the grips of a nefarious spell.
The plaintive screams of captive femininity
echoing through the autumnal fog.
Your heart racing as you push open the—let's face it—
unreasonably large doors of the Duomo.
The intertwining of diabolical flesh,
naughty nuns and perverted priests.
Johann Sebastien Bach's Toccata and Fugue in D Minor,
playing from the organ.
The sorcerer at the pulpit, bejeweled dagger aloft,
faithful Igor at his side.
The pure, virginal, damsel-in-distress tied—
ever so erotically—upon the sacrificial altar,
waiting for her 'Prince Charming' to rescue her.
Perhaps, already anticipating the many re-enactments
that await in the future, necessary to 'spice up'
the long years of Happily Ever-After.)
At least, that's how the Duomo feels from the street.

As you make your way
to the top of the Piazzale Michaelangelo,
all the hard edges of Florence soften.
Revealing a sun-drenched vista of terra-cotta rooftops
and lush, verdant green hills. The Duomo standing
triumphantly in the skyline,
a testament to mankind's culture and civilization.

Making your way down to the Arno river,
strolling through the manicured gardens of
Bardini and Boboli,
something changes.

The urban chaos across the Ponte Vecchio
isn't quite so disheartening.
Streets that once felt angry and rushed,
are now bustling and lively.
The newspaper stands
that earlier crowded the Piazza Sant'Ambrogio,
making their for a raucous terrazzo
where the locals can congregate,
enjoying an evening aperitivo.

You synchronize yourself with the pulse of Florence,
a real city filled with real people, living real lives.

And then, of course, there's David.

In my naïveté, I underestimated you, David.

Monument to perfection, the masculine ideal.
Not just corporeal, but spiritual, as well.

Would that I could be as strong and graceful as you, David.
Would that I could be as unwavering and timeless.
As pure and inspiring.
As noble and just.

Somewhere, in the dirty streets of my soul, you exist.
My higher self, my real self, my David.
—Firenze 2017

# THE ETERNAL CITY

A funny thing happened on the way to the forum:
I swore I saw Caravaggio brawling up in Monti.

Now, y—you might think I'm crazy, but, n—next: I spied
Titian, lounging with some gorgeous Venus-type on a
red divan at the Villa Spalletti Trivelli. A—And then I saw
Michelangelo—still as disheveled and shaggy as ever—
on the terrazzo of the Cafe della Pace, scribbling
in his notebook, while Peck and Hepburn tear past him
on a sky-blue Vespa, tra-la-la, la-la.

This cannot be happening, I think. It must be a trompe-l'oeil
brought on by Spritz and sun. But I am soon awoken
from this reverie by the most extravagant looking rascal—
the spitting image of Salvator Rosa—
who hands me a flyer—not (as you might imagine)
to 'the-best-carbonara-in-town,' oh no—but rather,
a prescription remedy for a dull intellect.
Screaming at every passerby in the Campo Di Fiori:
"Say something marvelous or shut up!"

Then, who do I run into b—but Anita Ekberg—
frolicking in the Trevi Fountain,
gold locks shimmering in the reflecting pools of water.
(Not pruney at all after all these years!)

N—Now, I know I'm going mad.
"The Vatican." I say, "My only hope is the Vatican.
"The Vatican will be my salvation!"

B—But would you believe: who do I see walking
through those haloed halls, but the angelic face of Raphael!

Now I'm thinking, what's going on here, anyway?
I—I mean: what's with all these Pope Johns and Piuises
and Clements and whatnot.
Maybe, th—they're all vampires!

N—Never dying, j—just t—taking turns behind the wheel!
An— And that's why they call it the Eternal City.
It's the Vampire City! That's what it is!
Hey...tha— That's why they needed so much
of Julius Caesar's blood!

Hoping to calm my nerves, I order a bottle
of Amaro Montenegro at Cafe Canova.
Commence trying to drink myself back
into a state resembling sanity.
But it seems that I have gone too far.
I am trapped now in a world of my own invention.
Spurring it on, in morbid delight.
I envision Federico Fellini at the table beside me,
Marcello Mastroianni—still as cool as ever,
sporting his midnight-black Persols, way past sunset—
Gina Lollobrigida and Sophia Loren on either side of him.
It seems they're enjoying a quick aperitivo of Campari on ice
before heading to Caligula's in Trastevere.
Everyone will be there: Elizabeth Taylor, Virgil, Petronius,
Bogey and Bacall, Anthony Quinn, Guilietta Masina.
It will be a Bacchanalia of blood
for these undead, immortal things.

And should I find it so strange, to be surrounded by illusions
in this city, so laden with history?

The Colosseum never far from one's thoughts
or geographical location?

Strolling down the Via del Corso, I watch the girls
in their high heels and dresses, shopping
in eternal reinvention without a care in the world
for what lurk in the shadows.

And why should they?

After all, it's just one more night in the Eternal City.
                    —Roma 2017

41

# LIDO DELLE SIRENE

Somewhere, in the quaint, crafted gloss
of patterned ceramiche, fried fish, and lemon gelato,
you lose yourself:
                    submit, surrender
to the sun, the rocky cliffs, the coastal villages.
To the pebble-strewn beaches
that burn your soles and test your balance.
Surrender
to the salty brine of the ocean
as it rests on your lips
and in the corner of your eyes.
Surrender to it all,
forgetting that you ever have to go back.
Forgetting
that this is only a brief and fleeting dream
along the strange curves of life's winding road.

And isn't life as beautiful and nauseating
as the serpentine roads along the Amalfi Coast?
Isn't life as sublime and untouchable
as those cliffs that jut up around you?
As unforeseeable as the horizon of the sea?

And yet, one day, you do wake up—
your inner tide sweeping you up into its swell—
and you are left with only the memories of lemons.

Lemons as large and mysterious as the moon, herself.

Lemons you never tasted but will,
one day.

        A promise you make to yourself,
        a vow you make to the moon.
                    —Amalfi 2017

42

# TWIN EAGLES SOARING

I have had the strangest day.

Waiting for the subway, I watched two men talking.
One of them stood on their tip-toes the whole time,
positioning themselves so the other couldn't see.
Then, when I got off the train, I came across a performer
juggling oranges in the street,
and as I passed, I heard a thud
and the most profound exclamation of defeat.

Now, for some reason I can't quite articulate,
I feel as though these two events are related to me.
That the universe is sending me a message.

Am I trying to stand taller than I am?
Am I overreaching my own ability?
I recall how you love Alden Nowlan's poetry:
the pure honesty of it.
                  He was my hero.
I wanted to write poems as simple and beautiful as his.
Have I strayed so far from that?

I feel like I'm lost and I can't find my way back.
I sit, listening to music and every song
speaks to me a little too much
and I'm afraid I'm losing you.

Yes, I'm afraid, but here's what I know:
I know that I love you.
I know when I look up into the sky
I want to see twin eagles soaring.
I know that when I look into my heart
I want to feel twin eagles soaring.

      One for the ways we love.
      One for the ways we laugh.

# THE ENDLESS KNOT

## I.

I'm scared that I am not doing enough.
That, at the end of all this,
you won't really have known me.

I want to share with you my trials and tribulations.
I want no secrets between us.

But perhaps, you would rather not draw back the curtain?
Perhaps, you would prefer me confined
to some predetermined limit of lines—no less, no more—
bland, undecipherable, anonymous.

What is it you wish of me?
Is it the poet or the poem you seek?

That is the impossible knot I am attempting to untangle,
yet, I fear, I may not be great enough for the task.

I live in a world of dreams.
Maybe, too much so.
But this life of bricks and roads...what else is there
but to escape? Somewhere, anywhere,
whatever small crevice of warmth and comfort available.

I dream of a wilderness
where the unfathomable gap between myself and...
god, goddess, cosmos...
                            is bridged, ever so slightly.
A union formed away from the constructed reality
of this ceaseless, quotidian assault—with its systems,
both myriad and intertwined. By equal turns
rational and oppressive; functional,
but not making any sense. Not to you,
to your human heart and cherry-blossom soul.

I wanted to write a poem entitled "The Endless Knot."
I became fascinated with the Shinto roots of Kinbaku,
the Japanese art of rope bondage,
and in particular, how it alluded to the use of shimenawa—
ropes made of hemp or straw used
for the ritual purification of sacred spaces.
It seemed to me an exquisite union of the sacred and profane.
How the seemingly violent act of sexual bondage
could be refigured as an act of purification and worship.
This led me down a long, winding path
where I began to seek out all the cross connections
and inferences that could be tied
to the knotty world of BDSM.

I conceptualized this poem as a pantoum;
attracted to the use of interwoven repeated lines
as a kind of form-follows-content play
with the image of the Endless Knot.
I had hoped to tie together a variety of disparate threads
including: the Eight Auspicious Symbols of Buddhism,
Tibetan Namkhas, Mexican Ojo de Dios,
the decorative arts of China, Islam, and Armenia,
Celtic knots and their roots to a pre-Christian polytheism,
mathematical knot theory and the untangling
of our genetic DNA, Indra's Net,
the etymological roots of Tantra,
dependent origination, eternal recurrence, Goddess worship,
mandalas, Neopaganism, and, of course, lest we forget:
the endless amount of fun you will have
tying your lover up in knots.

My only fear, was that—after all was said and done—
it wouldn't really amount to much.
Just another cold, dispassionate intellectual exercise—
too concerned with form and style—
that nobody would ever take the time to decode,
or comprehend.

Just a shrug of the shoulders and an eye turned
to more pressing matters,
more engaging comforts.
Forgotten, never to recur.
Itself, ironically, disengaged
from the karmic cycle of academic dissemination.
Perhaps, blissfully,
to have found some corner of Nirvana
reserved for works of art
removed from the purview of history.

      Finally at peace.
      Finally at home.

## II.

A blindfolded boy throws a flower upon the womb:
"Without love, there is only death and darkness—
an endless cycle from tomb to tomb,
the topology of whose curve none may deduce."

Without love, there is only death and darkness—
embrace his wrath as a revelation of wisdom,
the topology of whose curve none may deduce,
for the rainbow he binds you with brings freedom.

Embrace his wrath as a revelation of wisdom;
in the horror, the awe, the ecstasy.
For the rainbow he binds you with brings freedom
and you awaken a Pure Land of immortality.

In the horror, the awe, the ecstasy,
the world reveals to you its multitude of eyes
and you awaken a Pure Land of immortality
alive in the warp and weave of unseen skies.

# BOOTLEG SAKE

We were at Wasaga beach for summer vacation.
Staying there a few weeks, from what I remember.
I was still a few years away from touching, or kissing,
or falling in love, or any of that—shit,
it was July 1996, I was 13 years old.

I had forgotten my copy of Robert Silverberg's
The Man in the Maze
at the beach the day before
and when I went back to look for it,
somebody had thrown it into a fountain. Assholes.
I took it home and dried it out the best I could,
but I don't recall ever finishing it.
Come to think of it, I think they tore out
the last few pages, as well.

I think about that book sometimes.
Always look for it in the science fiction section
of used book stores.

While it was drying out
my dad took me to the corner store to buy some comics—
back when you could buy comics just about anywhere—
and that's where I found it:
my first issue of Heavy Metal Magazine.

I remember how strange I felt looking at that cover:
        this naked woman, eyes-locked
        over her shoulder, with this sinister looking
        liquid-metal alien behind her.

It wasn't erotic.
Or, I guess I should say, it wasn't sexy.
At least, not to me.
But it intrigued me.

I spent the rest of that vacation reading and re-reading
that copy of Heavy Metal—
up at night, everyone else asleep.

The stories were dark and funny and tragic.
I especially loved the main feature:
The Oath in Amber: The Amojar.

But it wasn't just the stories that captivated me.
Filling the pages between each story
were advertisements for stories even more illicit
and provocative than the ones published in the magazine.

A seemingly endless amount
of fantastic and forbidden pleasures:
      The Adventures of Druuna,
      Eva Medusa,
      Butterscotch,
      Young Witches,
      The Story of O,
      The Mercenary.

On and on it went.

I used to pore over each and every page
and ask myself:
          What were these stories?
          What happened in all these books?

It was a mystery
and I was enraptured.

Looking back, that summer was one of the happiest times
in my life:
      at the beach, in the sun, on vacation;
      Chinese food, science fiction, and comics.

Those days are over now, and not just my childhood—
that world that seemed so vibrant and endless
is now finite and quantifiable,
and all those publishers
that once populated the pages of Heavy Metal
seem to have faded into some lost horizon.

All the while that I was chasing the tangible,
the intangible was chasing me:
the internet arrives, and suddenly, there's no need
for forbidden things passed over counter tops,
wrapped in brown paper.

Prohibition is over, but I'm still thirsting for bootleg sake.

I get it: dirty comics don't sound quite so romantic
as Winchester rifles, wild horses, and the Westward frontier,
but there was something beautiful
in those strange, perverse narratives
and now they're gone.

Facility has won over aesthetic,
and I can't help feeling that we are helpless
against the unstoppable engine
of an increasingly utilitarian future.

The bad guys have won.
Or, at least they're occupying Casablanca.
And you without a Visa.

So have another drink at Rick's Café.
It's bootleg sake and Bogey's mixin'em strong.

II

# NOREASTER

The winter winds were rough, all told,
and many took their measure of the gale.
With scarce assurance from the blowing cold
found among the barren woods along the trail.

Nature, forsaking each to their own device—
whether hemlock bowed or sparrow's cry—
blew on, indifferent, for nothing else would suffice
except for tempest, full force, upon the land and sky.

Dark day followed by darker night,
one upon the other in perpetual gloom,
and whatever sorrows overtook the heart in fright
prevailed against Hope in this desolate Doom.

Shrouded such, as though engulfed in cloud,
I despaired that something had gone terribly wrong.
Never again would I hear aloud
the plaintive joy of the sparrow's song.

Till, lo, one morning, I awoke
with sounds of happy chatter on the breeze.
Spring had come and the storm broke
and blossoms alighted on budding trees.

I knew then that my wish had come true,
and curse this vagrant soul that ever doubted.
I knew then that I was born anew,
for I felt my wings had sprouted.

# MY FATHER TAUGHT ME HOW TO DREAM

My father taught me how to dream—
the sailor always abroad
on some sunset horizon.
Who came home
and took me by the hand
and said, "I love you, son.
I have faith in you."

My father, who took me by the hand
and(laughing,singing,dancing)taught
me to ride a bike through

      'onetwothreefourfive pigeons just like that.'

My father, the poet,
who taught me to love recklessly.

Some fathers are hard,
and forge their sons with fire and anvil,

but my father taught me how to dream.
Who took me by the hand
in the darkest of nights
and said, "See, see that star?
It will lead you home.
Now go and roam,

I have taught you well."

# MY MOTHER TAUGHT ME HOW TO LOVE

My mother taught me how to love—
the dancer always moving
to some strange, new beat.
Who spoke in tongues
and taught me the beauty of the unknown.
Who taught me how to say,
"el destino es siempre."

My mother, who took me by the hand
and led me through steps
from far away lands:

one, two, three, cha-cha-cha.

My mother, the cook,
who fed my soul with a boundless appetite.

Some mothers are scared,
and hide their sons behind closed doors,

but my mother taught me how to love.
Who took me by the hand
and led me through pungent streets.
Who said, "Look inside
and you will never be lost.
Look inside, and you will find

the whole world is waiting."

## THE WORDS THAT HURT THE MOST
## (ARE THE ONES THAT KILL TO KEEP INSIDE)

When Prince died, that's when it began.
He was your favorite musician
and I couldn't help but think of you
whenever I threw Around the World on the turntable.
Later, when I got into Steely Dan,
I remembered the stories you told me
about listening to their albums in the dark
in your friend's basement.

I always yearned for an experience like that.
It seemed special and significant.
Like when you described
the best New Year's Eve of your life
drinking cheap beer and trying to eat
every type of potted meat
you could find at the grocery store.

You had it all figured out with your 1956 teal Buick.
You were like a father to me.
Though I never told you that,
and you were too hip to flaunt it.
Like when you took me out
in your rowboat at the cottage
and we looked up at the stars, everyone else asleep.
Me underage but still bumming smokes.
And you said how the only thing that frightened you
was the concept of an infinite universe.

Last summer, when me and Bianca
moved into our apartment, she played
"Black Cow," off her phone, and we danced
in the empty apartment.
Blessing it with the good years that were to come.
And somewhere, in that moment, you were there.

Ah Brent, you'd like her.
She laughs from the belly
and talks from the heart.
I keep telling her she'll meet you someday,
but, you know, shame is a funny thing.

When Julia left me, everything fell apart.
I ran away from Toronto
and ended up running away from everyone in it.
Julia's married now, with two kids.
Shit, even Jen got hitched.

When Cole and Ellis tracked me down
at a poetry reading,
I couldn't believe how old they were.
I knew it had been too long.
I knew I had to see you, all of you.

I'm sorry.
Two words I've been holding in for so long.

I know you'll forgive me.
Probably have already, years ago,

and I'm just the darned fool
who spent ten years of his life
away from the people he loves the most.

# WAY OF THE POET

Don't let them fool you—
the way of the poet is not the way of the warrior.

It is the resolute acceptance of life! Not death.

How easy it is to go through this world a ghost,
permeated with the acrid stink of the grave,
never feeling the warmth of the sun's embrace.
So much harder it is to skip, care-free, fragile heart,
dizzy in wonder, untouched
by the nebulous shades of dolor, encroaching all around.

Fool, they'll call you,
who dedicate yourself to Truth and Beauty.
But it is fools who count their coffers with rusted hearts,
divorced from the majestic beauty
of Nature's adolescent bloom.

Be one with the leaves and grass.
Stay pure as the flower's promise.
Remember always the sun and 'that moment,'
        whatever it is.

They will try to pit you against one another,
dangling their prize for the 'room at the top,'
but it is a mansion that makes monsters of us all.

Nothing to lose and nothing to gain,
yet we yearn for the spotlight, nonetheless.
Bathed in an incandescent light, oblivious
to the growing things all around.
How our blood is but worms and soil
and we must return one way
        or the other.

# TO THE VICTOR

"Judge not, lest ye be judged!"

That's what the 'good book' tells us, isn't it?
That we should hold back our judgement,
reserve criticism, treat one another
with fairness and equanimity.

But who's kiddin' fa?
It's a feckless endeavur, onie way ye slice it.

A frisson of moral sentiment
soon plagued with rust.

Like the roric dawn,
you feel it transpire through you—
attempt to grasp the commodious grandeur of its promise—
but soon, it dissipates into an entirely different day.

Like the en vogue coifs of yester year
its naive idealism feels dated and you must admit
(even if only to yourself) that:
to the Victor go the Spoils.

Ah, make no mistake,
it is a bitter pith to chew on,
but you savor it, like an Italian digestif;
let the robust complexity settle on your tongue,
as you process the subtle array
of gentian, orange peel, and cinchona.

For there is refinement even in defeat,
like the samurai who falls on his own sword,
like the band that kept playing on a broken down tub

in the middle of the Atlantic ocean.

# WHAT THE KIDS ARE LISTENING TO

Awake into the unbridled fury of this ever present moment—
hungry and alive.

     Dreams beyond the muck.
     Hopes beyond the toil.

Permanence? Perpetuity?
These are for the Immortals, ye brief and fading thing.

You can spend your whole life
attempting to create something that will live beyond you,
but in the end, it will always fade.
Nothing is timeless.
You will always be prisoner to this;
trapped on an island more perilous
than anything Papillon could conceive of.

You keep calling yourself Van Gogh,
but nobody knows what the hell you're talking about,
because the only thing that matters
is what the kids are listening to,
and it's never what it used to be.
Every generation tuned to a new song—
mysterious, alien, ephemeral.
Each Age a revolution,
and you a part of it like all the rest, don't fool yourself.

So you better be what the kids are listening to—
even for a day, even for an hour.
Because once it's over, that's it: you're over the hill, old hat,
a fossil, a dinosaur,
a forgotten superhero with a dusty cape
just waiting to get retconned back into the narrative.

And hey, who knows?
Grant Morrison has done crazier things.

# PLAY THE HAND YOU'RE DEALT

True: you will never be an astronaut,
but you never really wanted that, did you?

Be honest:
you wrote thirty years of self-loathing and procrastination
into your 'Book of Life'
and now you've got to deal with the consequences.

You've got to play the hand you're dealt,
even if you dealt it to yourself.
Especially so.

Like Milton, you consider how your light was spent
because now the real work begins.

Sharks have the sharpest teeth and they never stop moving,
so neither do you.

# THE WELL'S GONE DRY

Although with each passing day
the bucket descended ever deeper—
like all endings—
you were not prepared for it.

The soul is comforted by familiar landmarks,
but the body needs water.

So, you pack up and head for a new home.

It was good while it lasted,
and you'll always remember it fondly.

# CUT YOUR LOSSES

At some point,
you have to cut your losses
and accept defeat.

Looking back,
it's the ones who jumped ship early
that were smart.

Who put down their pencil crayons
and picked up a calculator.

We need them too, I guess.
Maybe, more so.
Certainly, their money-filled lives attest to that.

It's like you're on a train
and every stop people keep getting off, but not you.

Is that because you haven't reached your destination yet?
Or because you have nowhere to go?

The thought engulfs you like a dark tunnel,
reverberating in your brain

as you barrel towards the end of the line.

# MEMENTO MORI

## I.

Well, I guess it's time for my obligatory death poem.

"Thus passes the glory of the world..." and all that.

Although, it always struck me as a little morbid
to build the legacy of your life on death:

"Do Not Go Gentle Into That Good Night"

I get it. It speaks to people.
In a weird sort of way: it's a crowd pleaser.
My problem is that you can't exactly add anything
to the dialogue, now can you? Just regurgitate
the same old fears, anxieties and time honored clichés:

"Hey, who's going to pay for my carpe per diem!" &
"Tempus fugit-about it!"

"Remember that you have to die..."
Now that's one dark cloud of a phrase if I ever heard one.
Some Old Testament shit:
                        knocking on the Pearly Gates,
                        bespectacled, old codger
                        pulling out the ledger,
                        calculating the sum of your actions
                        and misdeeds, you shuffling
                        left to right foot—

for truly, my friends, Heaven is reserved
for only the choicest of VIPs.

However, if you believe in reincarnation (like I do)
the phrase should really be: memento renascitur.

"Remember that you have to be reborn."

These days, I'm more afraid of not being reborn a Deadhead
than I am of Eternal Damnation.

"Remember that you have to die."
As though I could forget.
As though I could even stop myself
from wondering what mysterious prize
my fumbling fingers will grasp
out of that black top-hat of Death.

Perhaps, you already know what that prize is?
Know things about me that I, in this moment,
am not privy to. All the twists and turns laid out
for you in biographical concision.

After death, it all just becomes history, doesn't it?
And here's me, not even done living—so much to do,
so much left undone—eager, wondrous, hopeful;
this: the best life any of us are ever going to get.

Who the hell cares what happens next,
after the Merry-Go-Round spins its last twirl for you alone?
It's not exactly like the carnival ever closes;
there's always a new batch of young, fresh-faced hopefuls
charging into the fray: listless, lustful, abundant.

All I know for certain: is that I have not even begun to live.
Dust I may be and dust I may return; but until then,

I plan to ride every roller-coaster this life has to offer.

## II.

Now is the time to dance, now is the time to sing;
footloose upon the earth, carousing in the air.
Follow the whispering heart, glide upon the gilded wing.

Fools may frown, go furious in their futile flying,
never to realize what dreams await those who dare.
Now is the time to dance, now is the time sing.

We wise few will not waste our days in winsome wandering—
heed the magic thunder, awake to the lightning's flare.
Follow the whispering heart, glide upon the gilded wing.

Rage may stoke the spirit of a sad, broken thing,
but rage is a ragged rhyme robbed of harmony fair.
Now is the time to dance, now is the time to sing.

The music of the spheres chimes. Are you listening?
Are you alive to the stardust in your eyes and hair?
Follow the whispering heart, glide upon the gilded wing.

Meditate on the mysteries, not the worshipping.
Pulsate in the divine: here, there, everywhere.
Now is the time to dance, now is the time to sing.
Follow the whispering heart, glide upon the gilded wing.

# INFINITE SURRENDER

Surrender to the infinite within.
It comes alive when you least expect it.
Do not waste your days in idle remorse,
shameful for that which you cannot account for.
Be ready.
Make alive the promise that is inside you.
If you sin, sin joyfully.
Shun anything that cannot be celebrated.
Because time is precious and carnivals are few.
Realize those smiles may never cross your way again.
Be grateful for the rainbows.
More will come.
If not for you, then for others.
This world must become better.
We were born to surrender.
Surrender to the infinity within.

# LOVE & WAR

When the verdict finally came in,
I had to tip my hat to the winners circle.

Dice loaded.
Cards stacked.
Wheel gaffed.

But as they say:
all's fair in...

# SCHISM

Strangely, it was I who found myself in the land of Nod,
so far east of Eden. Although, then again,
I always did fancy myself the James Dean type.
Maybe that's why I never learned how to drive—
too much karmic baggage—nevertheless enchanted
by the smooth lines, mechanical prowess, and primal roar.
And, of course, nobody could say
they didn't notice my mark, could they?

How many years have I found myself transfixed here,
trapped in the lush sensuality of a Rubens painting—
your hand gripped around my throat, dagger poised
dramatically aloft—I naive, as you cunning:
"Come, let us go out into the field..."
It is a strange dance we find ourselves in, and I stumble
and falter, not knowing the secret combination of steps
as you pirouette to ever higher stratas of fortune and fame.
But I ask: what may flourish in this desert of abundance?

I won't condescend you with accusations of infernal pacts,
for we both know who the magician is between us.
It was doubtless a mundane decision, brought on by
rational deduction; a mathematical formulae involving
risk and reward, ledgers and balances and all the things
I abhor, but how many nights must be spent
polishing away the guilt?

I would dramatically implore: "Et tu?"
But what's the use? You can't get blood from a stone.
I would grope at contrived tropes like:
"You'll get yours." and "The meek shall inherit the earth."

But to what avail?

A Canadian won't have any trouble on that frozen lake,
      will they?

69

# DARKNESS IN HAVANA

There is darkness in Havana.
There is darkness in Havana.

In crumbling opulence, I roamed the rubbled avenues—
broken promises littering the streets, oppression
suffocating the air—haunted zombie-eyes trailed after me
down shadowed alleys, murky alcoves...
caliginous doorways...tortured metal beasts screamed past,
into a black and godless night—the agony
of their chthonic spew heavy in the air.

Trapped in this Cimmerian odyssey,
all thoughts of paradise quickly receded;
fading, like the memory of sand, surf and sea; waning,
like the promise of youth; now decayed
into that same apparitional decadence; now cursed
to that same entropic nightmare.

I was lost. Blind fool that I was, I couldn't see.
Wound up, afraid, plagued by anxiety and apprehension
and doubt—I couldn't feel where my steps were leading.
I couldn't sense what lay ahead. I couldn't know
that my wayward sojourn was always to you.
Again and again and again, this river of my soul
runs always to you.

I was adrift in an ocean of darkness,
then, suddenly, I arrived into the light.

Capoeira was born in Brazil
but came alive in my heart in Cuba.

Bewitched by the dizzy violence of limbs,
the pulse pounding of rhythm,
the undeniable choir of spirit,
I felt, finally, the Cuban soul.

That fighting, dancing, singing soul
which yearns to be free.
That rebel soul reveling in perseverance.
That vibrant soul who electrifies the night,
electrifies the darkness,
shining a light across the vast infinity of pain.

Oh yes, there is darkness in Havana.
But watch how the stars shine bright,

shimmering transcendence in silhouetted foment.

# PAY TO PLAY

Feast your eyes on rampant, unbridled, depravity—
impoverished by a lack of shame,
a sunken treasure, lost, no X to be found,
"Land ho!" however you may, me maties.

      "Silence! Ye bleeding, trampled thing!"
      The gods say.

But do I heed the relentless chitter-chatter
of their argle-bargle, bogus show?

      No.

I want to want to skirt the horizon
between the potential and possible.

I want to claw myself to the precipice of the next level
and stare down at the magnitude of all that I have passed.

To forge ahead, ever onward
to new adventures and greater plateaus.

Take me to the bleeding edge...
I am ready for a new paradigm.

But what's this, I see?
The countdown already begun?

And me with my pockets, once so full of quarters,
now vestibule for naught but lint and crumpled refuse...

It hardly seems fair.
Barely begun and it's ending already.

Don't get me wrong: you gotta pay to play
and I knew that from the start.

Thought I could play my own game—
make up the rules up as I went along—
but the fact is:

        you either buy in or you're bought out
        and that's the way it goes.

And now, there's a voice in my head saying:

    "You're tragic, kid, but you got no guts
    and you'll never be Steve McQueen
    no matter how hard you try.
    Just a chump, hustling for chump change,
    always on the ropes, barely holding on,
    some people losing money, sure,
    but most knowing the score from the start,
    a born loser, who'd settle for a warm bed
    and a plate of spaghetti.
    Just another apple-knocker from Apple-Knocker Land
    and there's more where that came from, son,
    believe me."

And the countdown ticks: 3, 2, 1...
as I reach into my pocket,
frantically fish out another quarter,
pop it in and press Start.

Cause, you gotta pay to play,
and I ain't finished yet.

# DANCE FOR YOUR SUPPER

'Forever' is an obtuse construction
made for feeble minds
as they rush through labyrinths of cruel, unfeeling men!

Go on, fill your field of vision with rainbows and butterflies,
but there ain't no pot of gold waiting for you
on the other side—not even a pot-eu-feu—
and if you want to eat,
you've got to dance for your supper!

Me? I'm just a rude boy
and don't mind skanking, no matta da tune!

Atten-hut!

I'm calling all you palookas, bindlestiffs and colporteurs.
Who's gonna join this callithumpian army?
Toplofty best be hiding when this scofflaw a' march
cause then: "The harder they come..."

Babylon come knocking but I absqualate to the shadows
cause the hero don't die till the last reel
and the film's still spinning:

projecting 35mm revolution
in the darkened theatre of your mind.

# BUNKER HILL

It's time to get out of my own way.
Let things happen.
Be more open.
Take it as it comes.

They say every dog has his day,
but I feel like I have been chasing my own tail
this whole time.

You can get so mad
that you stop seeing the world,
trap yourself in this perpetual conflict of
"They" and "We."

I bluster from the enceinte
of my self-inflicted fortress of exile,
laying siege to a world
that has not given me my due.

And yet, my artful machinations
blow up in my face
and the harder I fight, the greater I lose.

Rendering any victory
I might have achieved
a pyrrhic one.

For, you see,
Bugs Bunny always wins

and like Yosemite Sam, I must concede:

"I'm a Hessian without no aggression.
If you can't beat'em, join'em."

# THE COTTAGE AT THE END OF TOMORROW
## (for Rudyard Fearon)

When the present became too unbearable,
I sought refuge in both the past and the future.
Enveloped them around me
like an old, familiar quilt
against the deep winter chill.
But nothing is either made nor lost
in the cottage at the end of tomorrow.
It is merely a refuge from the elements.
A respite from the work-a-day struggle
of sad, restless humanity,
and, eventually, the land needs tilling,
the lawn mowing.
So I threw off my blanket
of worn-out mythologies—
subjecting life and limb
to the perils of the rain and snow—
to enter, once again,
into the land of the living.
Because, I had promises to keep—
promises written in the stars, carved in the cosmos—
to finish the Book already written
at the beginning and end of Time.
My path is strewn with regrets, remorses,
they obstruct my steps on this road not taken.
But I know, in my heart,
I must eventually arrive
into that glorious metropolitan of Now.

# THE LAST NIGHT ON EARTH

Outside, silver waves cascade on a coral sea,
sheltering palms rustle in the wind,
a blue moon and bright stars shine down,
there is magic in the air tonight on this:
the isle of dreams.

Inside, the band plays on,
protected by the gods.
Waterfalls and bird calls mix
with the sounds of steel guitar and vibraphone.
Driftwood and flotsam hang from the walls,
seashells and pufferfish lamps beside them.

Humphrey Bogart greets you in a white tuxedo.
Sinatra, Presley, and Lana Turner rub shoulders
in the jostling crowd.
Waiters rush by with ornate cocktails housed
in opulent 22 ounce snifters,
decorated in a profusion of orchids,
miniature umbrellas, and citrus.

Whether doe-eyed goddess or strapping god...
love will find you tonight.

This could be the last night on Earth.
You are lost in a rhapsody of rum,
intoxicated in the joys of exotic abandon,
surrendered to the lullaby of escape:

a sweet, soothing tonic
to relieve the chaos of a crumbling world.

# OUT WITH THE OLD

I have had my fill of dead and dying things.
In ages past, I sung to the glory of conquering kings—
immortalizing their reign in rarified song—
only to watch their kingdoms crumble to dust,
like autumn leaves blown to the wind.
Oh, I have had my fill of dead and dying things.

I have had my fill of dead and dying things.
Time and again, I praised the beauty of a doe-eyed lass—
celebrating their splendor in verse—
only to watch their vibrancy wilt away
like a cut rose in a vase.
Oh, I have had my fill of dead and dying things.

I have had my fill of dead and dying things.
I beseeched mankind to follow its higher self—
aiming the arrow of its thought towards a spiritual horizon—
and yet, how many dying hands grasp at gold,
while their life blows away like sand?
Oh, I have had my fill of dead and dying things.

Ages and ages, I have lived in this world,
the memories of it haunt the halls of my mind.
This pantheon of ghosts unwilling to take
their decorous adieu, despite the party being over.
My closets crammed with their moth-ridden rags,
while I, adorned in last years fashions, long
for more novel vestments.
To attire myself in the latest digs:
modern, hip, and chic.
                              A man about town.

I would not force them out into those cold midnight streets,
for even so, I hold their friendship dear.
But, alas, I have no more room in this cramped abode
and as the adage goes, it must be...

# THE SNAKE

I am something new today.

What this is, is not yet certain.
What is certain, however,
is that I am kinder, gentler, holier.

Each night I die and am reborn.
Each morning I rise anew.
Ready for the work ahead.
Replenished, contented.

Sloughed off is the dead skin of my past self.
That tired, worn thing.

That which has no use, I discard.
Only to shine brighter
in the coming dawn.

Gilded in a skin which knows no death,
only life

and the living that awaits it.

# SELF-PORTRAIT

I am an island; words in the stars; dark leaves overhead...

And I remember the days when...
your hands like petals, my voice
cracked, plaintive, pleading—

we realize this breath, and this breath only—

The sun, moon, and stars are lost;
I find only your lips, your breasts.
This ever present knowing, who in what I was...
as though I thought I could hold the moment
like sand in a glass—

Bathe in the sunlight of angels.
Touch the flaming Heart-of-Now.

These dreams are for you alone.
All art is everything. Abandon. Enter.

You nibble at my skin.
Your soul is the exact colour of sunsets,
your eyes like mythology.

I scattered my soul through the never of folding clouds,
saw all the hate that was black in my heart...

"I dream of trees under this ocean mud
and flowers bloomed as such that I could map the world
in your name and voice."

But I will miss your brightness tomorrow.
The beautiful wounds we cherish most dearly
are those which do not heal ever, really, fully, completely.
Those words outside of language.

Could it be gone? The dreams, my dreaming land of yore?
Spent gift and the gods all crying...

I sought the river of dreams:
scuffed knees and rainbows forever;
the midnight shower of stars;
the endless discovery...every blade of grass.

Your eyes are stars.
You awake in me a blue-wash ocean wave.

There are doorways everywhere that I want to open.
Reflect you and me.

Where does it all begin?
Where does beginning begin?

Thought back to dreams and clouds...
in truth, it was infinity.

# ISLAND OF THE BLEST

I sat down and read
every poem I had ever written.

Tried to remember who it was that wrote them.
Go back...
       not to innocence perhaps, but somewhere...

How did I come to this point in time?
When did it all get so strange?
Progression? Continuity?
What are these abstract fictions?

I feel lost,
       adrift from a past that feels so unbearably far.

Are the poems enough to guide me home?

There is so much I left out in them—purposely cryptic—
and now, they are all that I have left.
They are both my loci and imagines
as I wander the ruins of my mind
in search of a 'Palace of Memory.'

But memory is not a structure you can visit at will,
more an 'Island of the Blest,'
a utopia you'll never quite discover,
(mixed opinions as to its latitude and longitude)
residing, somewhere,
in the sea of your mind...
and you, little more than pirate,
plundering what treasures break to the surface.

I close my eyes and dream of that island—
the beaches, the sand,
the cold, cool drinks
crowned with miniature umbrellas.

I have been sailing so long,
and my feet yearn to touch solid ground.

"Landlubber," they'll call me
and I'll laugh
and tears will stream.

"Home," I'll say,
"I have found my home."

# ACKNOWLEDGEMENTS

Some of the poems in this manuscript have previously appeared in *Vallum, Graphite Publications, Dreamers Creative Writing,* and *Big Windows Review.*

# BIOGRAPHICAL NOTE

Devon Gallant is the author of five books of poetry: *The Day After, the flower dress and other lines, His Inner Season, S(tars) & M(agnets),* and *Bootleg Sake.* His work has been previously published in *Vallum, Carousel,* and *Dreamers Creative Writing.* He is the publisher of *Cactus Press* and the co-host of the bilingual reading series *Accent.* He currently resides in Montreal.

# LIST OF POETRY READINGS & ESSENTIAL APPEARANCES BY DEVON GALLANT

**Lawn Chair Soiree — Sept 16th 2021**
*Montreal, QC*

**Visual Arts Centre Reading Series — Jan 26th 2020**
*Montreal, QC*

**Words & Music Festival, Westmout Park — Aug 11th 2019**
*Montreal, QC*

**The Argo Bookshop Reading Series — Aug 8th 2019**
*Montreal, QC*

**Lawn Chair Soiree — May 16th 2019**
*Montreal, QC*

**Spoken Word Paris — Oct 8th 2018**
*Paris, France*

**Vallum Magazine Launch — April 29th 2018**
*Montreal, QC*

**Vallum Magazine Launch — April 27th 2018**
*Toronto, ON*

**Blue Coffee Reading Series — Aug 18th 2014**
*Toronto, ON*

**Kafein Bar — June 17th 2014**
*Montreal, QC*

**Art Bar Reading Series — April 22nd 2014**
*Toronto, ON*

**The Yellow Door Reading Series — Feb 20th 2014**
*Montreal, QC*

**Spoken Word Paris — Various Appearances, Feb-Sept 2013**
*Paris, France*

**livewords — Nov 1st 2012**
*Toronto, ON*

**livewords — Nov 12th 2008**
*Toronto, ON*

**Carousel/Lantern Magazine Launch — July 3rd 2007**
*Toronto, ON*

**Diamond Cherry Reading Series — June 18th 2006**
*Toronto, ON*

**St. Clair Art Walk Street Festival — Oct 1st 2005**
*Toronto, ON*

**Ellington's Cafe — Sept 15th 2005**
*Toronto, ON*

**Art Bar Reading Series — Feb 2005**
*Toronto, ON*

**Diamond Cherry Reading Series — Nov 15th 2004**
*Toronto, ON*

**Art Bar Reading Series — Aug 17th 2004**
*Toronto, ON*

**Syntactic Sunday — July 11th 2004**
*Toronto, ON*